TO

_____

FROM

_____

HIRAETH

FAIRYAL ALLYBOCUS

leaf
publishing
house

PREFACE

"Hiraeth" is a Welsh abstraction of a homesickness for a home to which you cannot return, a home which you may have never even been to. It is the repository of all that could have been, your hopes and dreams, the nostalgia, the yearning, the grief for lost places, times, and people. It relates to the unfathomable moments which have disappeared without warning, as a cruel reminder of the things that matter and which touch your inner soul long enough to leave a permanent scar. It lives on doggedly in your memory, and all efforts to remove the trauma and the rare, sweet moments of ecstasy and fulfilment remain futile, because time changes everything, pain and pleasure becomes embedded in one's marrow. It is also associated with the bitter-sweet memory of an era, a person, a time, while being grateful for their presence and the ambivalence of your own experience.

This book is a collection of poetry of the longing for a time which has gone forever, and the reminiscence of the good old days that one won't get to see again. It will describe the feelings that bloom in love lost and abandonment, the stages in finding closure on your own and regaining one's strength, fortitude and spirituality.

On a personal level, I have grown to believe that suffering in all its aspects is inevitably an integral part of the human condition. In the labyrinths and circumstances of my life, suffering has been an impetus for my transformation, both mentally and spiritually- It contributed to expand my consciousness in a way to help me live a better life with greater composure. Consequently, through this book, I have weaved words around feelings and thoughts, as an attempt to empower people who, having been abandoned without concerns or care, are seeking some light in order to get out of the profound darkness of unexplained desertion, people who are trying to regain their self-confidence so that they learn to stop making excuses for the boorish behaviour of others, they learn that heartbreak, disappointment and agony can be transformational, as the broken down metamorphoses into the wholesome and flourishing again. In other words, every weakness, every let-down, every callous effort on one's integrity does not need to cripple, but instead it pushes one to draw on his/her inner strength and moral vibrancy when facing the coldness of rejection where once only ease and comfort used to be.

The fundamental aim of this book is to help lessen the sufferings of vulnerable orphans of Syria in this terrible war. In this regard, all royalties received from the sales of the book will go towards a charity to improve the quality of life of the orphans. To note: **This is not for any promotional purpose.** I work as a volunteer for that particular charity and so, in good faith, I would hope for the orphans to have the benevolent support of all you generous souls out there.

I've buried graveyards of memories inside me
to such depths that no force can uproot them.
Yet again, I constantly find myself digging for the strength
to write about their burdening meanings.

CONTENTS

A PERENNIAL ACHE

Warbles and embroidered blooms unfurl an enchanting spell.
The dusky flush of nightfall glistens across the tenebrous manor,
embracing the verdant floor in a cold cradle.
Memories waft around the imbued aura-
Bleed a perennial ache of a foregone time.
Vivid shades of melancholy seep in this treasured land
filled with recurring nostalgia,
reaching for the opulence of an incomplete story,
incomplete talks,
incomplete dreams.
Like the lack of synchronicity of some days between twilight and shadow.
Like a nimbus without its defining halo-
The clouds are incomplete too.
The weather is not the same as it used to be.
The wind seems halted.
The earth does not meet the sky.
An elusive essence of incompleteness lingers in these days.
Though they have evolved,
Goodness knows-
When in a moment of ardent ecstasy,
will they all be complete again.

APOCALYPSE

The sun is going down.
The lake's dried up.
The trees wince in pain.
Flowers halt their blooming.
Time is frozen between the jaws.
My heart is frostbitten.
My wounds are telling stories.
And my days are forged in darkness and fear.
I am sad, like the setting sun in the winter sky.
Desperation expands in my chest, until I can't breathe anymore.
I keep fighting for a place to call home.
I am alive but I have left my life behind.

Time stood still.

She dolefully came face to face with her lugubrious fate.

But could she ignore the pestilent quagmire of her past,

the secret heritage she had yet to reveal

and the irresistible urges of her own insufferable wounded

heart?

FLASHBACKS

Eyes closed, we venture with trepidation into a streaming
timeline of memories.
Little bits of our soul dwell in the places we know so well,
with those people who once mattered,
in songs that once shimmered our hearts,
smells that suffused our souls,
the feelings we once cherished-
They are captured within us and come back to us in flashbacks.
Time is cruel, and leaves parts of ourselves behind.
Memories and faded scars are like ghosts of the past-
Strumming through the loose strings of a bygone era,
we coerce ourselves through that eidetic door,
of words so untrue,
disappointments and regrets,
acrimonious recollections lurking deep
that refuse to stay buried,
the pictures dance in our heads.
Some merely exist to relive,
and others are meant for painful lessons learned,
only to be reminisced with despair at the unrepentant
callousness.
But miraculously, out of this puddle of rues-
We are born with such resilience;
to morph those wistful flashbacks,
into idyllic bliss.

I WAS HAPPY

A bonfire sealed the beginning of the summer night.
I lied supine on that hammock,
staring at the wonder above me,
a boundless night sky,
full of twinkling stars.
The glorious moon shone its beauty upon the sea water.
I fell asleep talking to you.
When I woke the next morning
to the sweet mellow hues of the morning sunshine,
swaying palm trees,
the feeling of crisp sea breeze on my face,
the sounds of gentle waves crashing to the shore
and seabirds chirping-
You were there,
within the far away landscape,
but still close to my heart.
And in that moment,
I was happy.

His heart was frosted cold.
because I couldn't live without him.
So now I keep on weaving odes on tapestries,
an embroidery of words
in a fabric of conflicting emotions
of crossing blue sapphire and ruby colours-
In the hope of stitching together,
canvas of my heart.

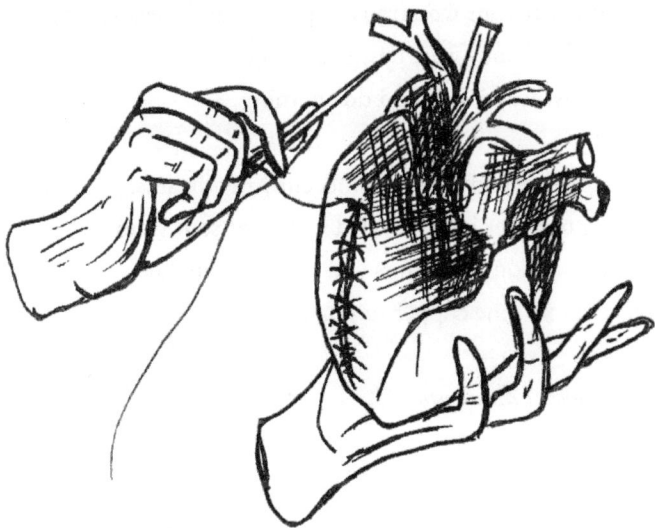

TRACES OF YOU

I tried my best to erase all traces of you.
Clear edged remembrances to plunge me through.
How you used to be, what you meant to me-
Before you left me with nothing but burns of third degree.

My mind is now an archive of your song recordings and voice.
Each plays on repeat, kindling my agony-filled heart to rejoice.
Your pictures, your arts from summer gone settle in my eyes-
Drawing me back to the days of laughter and coloured hair
dyes.

Tell me how can I forget your beautiful face and seraphic smile?
I marveled at your wondrous fine weave and elegant style.
Your skilled hands were desires stirring-
I was convinced you could do anything.

After all these nights, you still occupy my dreams.
Basking together in untraveled worlds or so it seems.
My imagination still paints you my favourite hue.
You've stained me copper sulphate blue.

- Time doesn't dilute you.

I ambled into the woods.
Steeped in wild beauty, where loneliness broods.
Canopy of trees, sun rays falling on the rugged path-
To the soft, soothing breeze, I confessed wounds of the
aftermath.
And into the wobbling rustle of leaves-
Scattering golden umbrage to its eaves,
I whispered,
and wept,
and wished that I could say it all to you-
Starting with 'I miss you.'

SPLENETIC MEMORIES

The shadows of the past have come to rest here.
Splenetic memories of what you said come blazing through my mind.
They keep recurring fiercely,
engulfing my entity in a vortex of torment,
leaving me wishing you would return to break them off.
Yet, even if I hang my wishes on the wall of serendipity,
not a tiniest beam of light would come far behind that wall.
For you are gone beyond recall-
And I am devastated beyond belief.

THE RECALL

In the hardest times of my life,
when the days were dark,
the nights were long and cold
and the sky was mourning a bitter lament-
You stood amidst the chaos and earthquakes.
The comfort of your presence patiently waiting
for my rebirth from the broken pieces of my heart.

Though-

You were my oasis,
the ever present well of stillness and natural ease.
You were the balm to my broken soul
and the lamp of hope which brought radiance to my world of
darkness.

You were something, until-

You started to drown me.
Your bitter words numbed my soul.
Your flame singed my heart.

And suddenly

I was suffocating, gasping for breath.
I grew weary and drained.

I began to wander aimlessly, searching for the light that had gone.

But

No matter which path I'd take, which trails I'd follow,
all the roads pitilessly led to you-
Like I was destined to keep toiling on your heart of stone.

RENAISSANCE

As her woebegone fate spun its web of doom and dismay,
she was comforted with the thought that
she had left her dangerous ordeal behind.
She yearned to tell the world of the slings
and arrows of misfortune that had left
a trail of dismay and pain
on her munificent heart.
Buoyancy and positivity,
her faithful and loyal companion in arms,
washed away the residual pain and heartache.
She made her vow that no interloper would ever breach
her walls of comfort and self-esteem.
Revenge is a dish best served cold
and the coldness in his icy heart will freeze over
the piercing reality that life is much better-
When her heart remains open to the good generous souls,
waiting to take her on an exquisite journey of enlightenment.
A renaissance she had always desiderated.

TRAPPED

Like a gust of wind, you swooped into my life.

Only to evanesce as soon as I got a handle of your sight.

Like a fallen leaf, I lost sense and spirit of my existence.

Seared with a blast of grief, unable to cope with the distance.

I was left in an empty bosk, trapped in the web of seasons that pass.

Along with your memories hanging as drops of dew, upon the blades of winter grass.

Eons have passed since I've lived-
As though the spirit is still bound to the body but the breath
has ceased.
The longing of missed moments impart-
As though a jeremiad is buried inside the heart but the arcana
slowly depart.
I may be cursed to such vehemence-
As though the soul yearns for what once was but shudders to its
imminence.
I keep thinking about you all the time-
As though your memory scourges but dwells in every breath of
mine.

YOUR CRUELTY

Bear what you can.
What you can't,
leave it to your lord-

Coming from you,
reassuring and holy,
until the truth was so transparent.
You killed me first.
Do you hear me?
You killed me first before I could walk, talk, breathe, shriek.
Before I even knew the rules of the world and yours.
Your cruelty travelled through the back of my spine like a bolt
of lightning.
And all I could do was blink.

You're the one heartless, loathsome and odious.
Don't you see?
There's blood dripping from your hands like rain from an
upturned sky.
You are the devil in disguise who meticulously designed words,
to be spitted onto me like poison.
Oh how you pelted me with the unbearable;
inflicted without responsibility so that you can walk free,
leaving me shackled without mercy,
to the pain and misery.

- The lord will not clean your mess.

You promised me that I would find a better man than you-
As a betoken of what I deserve.
But I never aimed to settle for any less when I chose you.

- Who sees the rose and plucks its thorns instead?

EMOTIONAL VOID

Have I arrived to the emblem of your throne?

Or have I lost my itinerary in the abyss of the forgotten?

My crying heart can't but sip this caustic emotional void.

Even upon wishing, you can't come back-

As you are a bygone time.

But these memories have kept you like a flower inside a book.

You shall remain in my heart and fragrant in my breath forever.

REPRESSION

Your atrociousness unreasonably tore a heart.
But here it is beating amply and proudly.
Your rancor left a struggling soul in utter misery.
But here it is willing to live,
and ache for the repressed chronicles of a lost fairytale-
The repressed words of a lost conversation;
the repressed thoughts of a lethargic story of the past;
the repressed feelings of true love.

THE HONEYSUCKLE AND THE HONEYBEE

Warm evenings speckle in the lily pond
amidst the marshy pasture.
Air so poignantly redolent with-
Spring blossom of dewy moisture.

Giving way to the gilded honeysuckle
holding nectar of crystalline amber.
As it sways effortlessly,
the golden honeybee beckoned upon its frail limber.

Whence, tenderly paving its path in,
fervent to every flowery fragrance.
Thence armorously filling its glassy cell with-
 Sweet nectar of blossom's inheritance.

There I stood in awe, at the peak of the arbour,
brimming with matchless bliss.
Absorbed by the sight which touches my thoughts,
with wonders such I miss.

Endless desires cast upon continuous ripples,
spreading with every wish I dream upon.
A radiant allure washing down on me,
luscious and burning reminders of a time forgone.

ICE CASTLE

Beyond the sea and far away,
a million miles from our town.
Beneath the night sky,
where coloured lights reflect off
ice pillars on majestic glaciers
and crystal domes are glistened with
the luminescence of the moon.

The footsteps of my empty heart
beckons me here.
I don't recall the first time we stepped inside.
But the last time we left,
it occurred to me how exactly a heartbreak feels.

Since then the ice castle has collapsed.
Along with the chain of memories we made here.
It now sings the blues of our separation.

TIME IS AN ERASER

I sit under a street lamp,
evening breeze hugging my bones.
I ruminate about every teardrop wasted.
Every tale of woe pursued.
Every betrayal endured.
They will fade away.
I keep convincing myself-
Time is an eraser.
It will reduce them into forgotten dust.
My fist might try taking hold of illusions.
But at the end of the hour,
it would stop hurting-
Because it would not matter anymore.
The memories will fade away too-
Like vinous flavours fade in taste;
autumn leaves fade in winter;
and life fades to death.

MISTAKEN

I was mistaken.
I avow-
To expect you to carry my misery in your hands
was unreasonable for anyone to ask.

But you were not anyone,
you were the one I considered as my own,
the one who slaked my thirst for love and affection.

My soul was so parched,
and your hands seemed reasonable enough
to hold the sea of pain trapped inside my heart
and to fill my yearnings to the brim.

All seemed chaos.
Abruption and apparent blows.
Every corner of her mind felt like a warzone-
Invaded by whispers of a chaotic love.
Nothing made sense.
She was fighting a losing battle to save you,
besieged in an endless cycle of havoc.
However dangerous it seemed-
The warrior in her conquered every violent threat that came
into her path.
She faced both the ignominy of your people
and your explosive slanders
that burned her wounds into ashes.
She gathered every hope and resilience within,
until nothing was left to hold on.
So now let it be known-

She loved you too much and that was killing her.

OCEAN OF BAD MEMORIES

Floodgates have been flung open,
accompanied by nostalgia and 'what ifs'-
That line was a myth I loathed,
since it never ceases to put forth its heavy intensity.
Its weight increases with missed moments,
struggles against the flash floods of doubts
across the white-capped wishes and dreams-
Secretly hiding the salty reality mixed in,
inundating my mind in a whirlpool of 'what could have been'
swallowing my heart,
drowning every bone, every wish
and slipping on the sand of faded promises,
in the hope to breathe under the sea of potentials-
An ocean of bad memories hit me like a tidal wave.
But luckily I struggled to reach safe land,
where promises are sanctified with sacred oaths,
false hopes are never given
and dreams are made of seashells.

He loved the game of winning,
leaving blank spaces in each heart
and bits of soul that captured his attention.
This was good for his pride.
He was addicted to the feeling of being in control,
luring his star-crossed preys in,
parading them around his image.
They would lose themselves in the maze of his wildered ways.
He would then devour them whole and eventually spit them
out.
Until they were left with pieces of themselves, he can just
manipulate with.
It was a punishment he convinced himself they deserved,
for being weak enough to love him.

MOSAIC HER

Cracks and fissures carve their initials,
Upon fragments of brokenness over her soul.
Hopes and dreams shattered like broken crystals.
Sooth along these lines demise be her only dole.

An incoherence of blending scars and flaws.
Attuned to recklessness that left her colors to bleed.
Howbeit exhausted she was, grasping at straws-
In the quest of peace, intrinsic to the life she'll ever need.

Parts of her were distorted orders of a chaotic realm-
Finely indented in patterns of chaos as a token.
Susceptible to the doubts of the world sought to whelm.
How do you love someone so broken?

The way you would love an intricate mosaic-
Tis assembled of broken pieces and mayhem,
Composed of cracks and hues so frantic.
Still its beauty gleams like an exquisite gem.

When the night falls,

the stars dazzle the dark sky.

Birds have returned to their roosts.

The eyes are closed in deep slumber.

The kingdoms have closed their doors.

Extending moments meant for no one but deity.

When you unravel into frayed ends,

when agony storms into your body in cataclysmic tornadoes

and grief holds no mercy but holds all of your heart,

in nights like these,

endure with a beautiful patience.

A kind of patience that behoves a magnanimous person like you.

Stand before your Lord in worship.

Count your wounds.

Pour your tears on the prayer mat till dawn.

Behold-

Even though the wishes are still unadorned,

a different kind of peace will linger in the next morning.

And the day will hold a divine ataraxy.

STRAINS OF EXCUSES

Perfectly poised,
the lies you reasoned with for leaving were not only a
whitewash.
Darling,
when you guilefully portrayed your words in the most beautiful
canvas,
I could smoothly streak stains of excuses among the chromas.

OUR VENN

The love I gave you and the love I received back were two different circles that intersect.

The common area of intersection would have been our lucky union.

And I placed the bets against my jinxed fate to stand in it.

But nothing could warn me that your circle was empty the whole time.

YOUR ABSENCE

The space between my arms is closed
by the immensity of the void that replaces you,
in the hope of seeing you return.
Drowned little by little
by a newfound lucidity.
My mind tames storms during the day,
only to pour them onto my pillow at night.
Your absence deepens my gaping wounds.
I see the extent of my sorrow
but I cannot restrain it.
You were everything to me
and you left me with nothing.
To the abyss that crushes my heart
and accentuates my miseries-
You brought out the moon for me
at a time when I could see only darkness.
You who have made me known joy-
You are today the cause of my biggest sorrow.

The intoxication of our past moments has not gone from my
eyes yet.
My arms have not released your heavenly body yet.
Left on my skin by your lips, your breath is still there.
The feel of my fingertips tracing your cephalic vein, that dream
is still there.

OCEAN'S RHYTHM

Now gracing the sandy shores-
The feral waves crash to be redeemed.
Sea glass frost nearly gone;
overarching winter's requiem.
But if thou hearken to the ocean's rhythm-
Thou shalt recollect a symphony of truth.

If only I could pen down letters to you,
I would graciously tuck them in a time capsule-
Hoping you would read them in an afterlife.

Dear grandpa,
I would never know that there could be such a fine line
between life and death,
had I not seen you convulsing in your death throes,
when you showed signs of losing life at the hospital.
The most torrid times of my life was striking me at that time
and as I stood right next to you,
I felt pangs of agony crawl my spine and rip my heart,
overburdening my whole existence with the unending gloom of
your loss.
'I was not ready for this yet'-
I kept repeating to myself.

Dear grandpa,
I grew up with you by my side.
I devoted my life to achieving your dreams.
And one of them was yet to be fulfilled.
I wish I could apologize to you-
I am sorry I could not make it in time.
I am sorry I let the cruelty of the world immobilize me.
I am sorry I was not in good health.
There is nothing left inside me but regrets.

Dear grandpa,
I made a museum out of your room where I keep going back.
Your books, your bed, your chair, your glasses, your clothes-
They all remind me of you.
Your footsteps still echo in my mind.
I still hear your voice narrating tales of your village.
I wish I could tell you how your death cast a shadow over my
life.
I wish I could tell you how terribly I miss your nurturing love.
I wish I could tell you how awfully I long to feel the strength in
your hugs.

Dear grandpa,
You shaped my whole life.
But my life has been split between blessing and curse.
And your lessons have pulled me apart and together.
Maybe the last lesson you were meant to teach me is that I can
survive on my own.

Dear grandpa,
I may have lost you to another life entirely.
But your memory is etched deep in my heart and soul.
And your voice still has the same resonance of the profound
affection-
Which I felt every time you called me your princess.
Sharing your life with me fills me with gratitude and marvel.
I feel blessed that a man of honour like you was destined to be
my grandfather.

Dear grandpa,

Your soul has returned to where it belongs.

I pray that the peace of the good Lord remains with you till the end of time.

I hope to meet you somewhere in the heavens.

For now I have a trail of the good times that we made, lining my heart.

Thank you for all the memories;

They are all for keeps-

For good.

DEATH

You,
are mortal,
but not your life energy,
and definitely not your deeds.
Your soul,
once created
can never be lost,
nor dissolved.
It is only seized and released
from your body,
transferred to its next destination,
another world.
Life and death are in a constant of motion-
Just like energy, which is never destroyed,
but only continues to live on a quantum scale-
Death,
is not a momentum.
But a continuum.
Your flesh and bones
can be reduced to dust,
though you were not created to perish-
But to remain forever.
So, in light of this continuum,
you shouldn't enmesh your soul
in a myth-
By lusting for your own glory.

Nor should you write your own story.
In the end,
you can't have anything your own way-
Death will find you anyway.

SEA VIEWS

I revitalize by the dreams you poured into my eyes.
Sea views and baby blues.
By everything vibrant and pure-
Keeping me alive.

HEARTBURNS

I get heartburns now.
I try to press on my chest,
to ease this excruciating pain in my heart.
It intensifies with every breath that I cannot catch.
This suffocation eats me up from within
and my ribs begin to buckle.
They say the only way to bear a pain is to feel a greater,
immediate pain.
I think this is what my body does to help me cope with your
hostility.
I get heartburns now.

THE PAIN OF SURVIVING

You do not have to grieve gracefully.

Soak involuntarily in the uncomfortable lull of life.

Do not conceal it with magic and ruffle.

It is blood and pills,

sore muscles and heartaches,

sleepless nights and screaming into pillows.

Strive through it as it is-

Raw and fervent.

Do not shrug off the pain of surviving.

Along the wreckage that deepens between
experience and oblivion.
She casted her secret sanctuary amidst a primeval forest-
Where trees are rooted for ages untold,
and secrets still unfold.

THE LOVE I HAD FOR YOU

I wanted to make you feel like the love I had for you could be-
Your home.
A place to come back,
a place to feel safe,
a place to feel whole.
It was too glorious to be kept to myself.
So I tried to show you its beauty.
But instead you accused it to be insanity-
Wherefore burning it all down.
Tracked in shame,
grime,
and charred remains to its rubble.

The things I would do for you,
span oceans and lifetimes,
colours in amethyst nights,
blankest of spaces
and infinite matrices.

I'd tread unknown paths,
walk through storms,
settle into spirals of tribulation.
All for you.

In fact this is what I did.
But none of that meant anything to you.
You just could not give me back the one thing you took away
from me-
Peace.

DAMAGED-SHAMED-CONSUMED

*How do you stay safe in the hands of a brute without being
damaged?*

Her soul was seeking for his attention.
But she was somewhat his library book.
He checked her out for some time.
And left her wishing to be owned in poor shape.

*How do you fix an addiction to a forbidden fruit without being
shamed?*

Her body was longing for his presence.
But she was somewhat his roaming deer.
He stayed at the top of the tree like a forbidden fruit.
And hopelessly, she kept reaching for him.

*How do you escape from a hurricane of sweet temptations without
being consumed?*

Her heart was starving for his love.
But she was somewhat his Friday night girl.
He fed her some sugar-candy words.
And naively, she feasted on them.

INCONGRUITY

My heart was in fragments
but it was those of gold.
From this incongruity,
I could write about love
and still not feel it.

IN THE FLAMES

You kept me in the flames to be reduced to ruins.
And as the blaze rose higher,
strewing over-
You burned with rage and hate.

Half a decade in,
that was all the time
it took me
to pull the loose strings
of your transient
fake love.
Had I known
a little earlier that
your mercurial heart
was not a silky drapery
for strong bonds,
I would have saved
my staunch heart
from an epithet of
poison laced needles.

AN ODE

"And Peace be upon him the day he was born and the day he dies and the day he will be raised up to life."

His birth was a miracle.
The Lord Himself picked his name.
He was a pulse of an angel-
An epitome of purity-
A graven image.
Nobly created and flawless.
Righteousness, compassion, strength.
His attributes were saintly honourable.
Loyal to his purpose since childhood-
To love and serve God-
He lived in seclusion.
Adored even by the devil-
He was a halo of glory.

To the one who reached the doors of Jannah- You are the reason
why my eyes cry more tears than raindrops fall from the skies.

Tonight I belong to another era-
As I cry my heart out with desperation.
My stuttering breath comes in gasps.
Pain clawing at my stomach-
From the weight of your tragedy.
You paid a heavy price for preaching against evils.
Blood stained over your tender soul.
Woe to the wretched woman who asked for your head.
How heinous she could be-
Even your assassin must have drawn sharp breaths at her
gruesome request.
Your holy head brought to her on a platter;
spoke out in a moment-
"She is not lawful for you."
Still truthful, still staunch, with heaven keys.

My glorified seraph-
You did not die in vain.
The earth swallowed her body in vengeance.
The skies were red, mourning over your death.
The heaven wept for you.
Your selfless courage is your creed's triumph.
Your sacrifice is embedded in our hearts.
And your sacred scriptures are eternally observed-
So sleep peacefully in your abode.

YOUR MESSAGES

I have safekept your messages
as proof.
One day I will teach my daughter,
how words,
honeyed as can be-
mean naught,
without honest intent.
And how words,
heart wrenching as can be-
may destroy the soul,
leaving everlasting scars.

WOUNDS

She left her raw wounds exposed to him,
and all he could do was rub salt onto them.
Utterly oblivious,
that the girl who can bear to have salt on her deadliest wounds,
it is hardly possible to terrify her with more salt.

You could dissect her
beyond saving,
she would still go back
to her roots
and
grow flowers
in her wounds.

A MOMENT IN THAT DAY

There was a moment in that day,
when my breath was stolen-
For what felt like a lifetime,
but which in effect was fleeting.

There was a moment in that day,
when my heart was captivated-
For what felt like a destination,
but which in reality was a deadlock.

There was a moment in that day,
when my mind was relieved-
For what felt like an answered prayer,
but which in truth was a premonition.

THE PLAGUE

The mask of guard has fallen on a hysterical earth.
The lavish life that moved hearts has slipped away.
Meaningless seem to be the world's luxuries.
Trapped between life and death,
are chained souls,
with only hope to endure.
Every one dreads the causatum that is touched by hands.
Every inhale is an apprehension.
The days of halcyon dreams have perished.
And even despair has become vain to destroy.

The plague leaves the vulnerable feeble and languish.
With tenfold increased death day after day,
winged agony sweeps in many homes.
The kin grieves the loss of their loved ones.
Cruel death! Their conscience reproves them-
For being helpless.
Have no last gathering at their deathbed, no funeral.
Now do we learn to cherish each moment,
regret the glorious days we once took for granted.
Now do we reflect on our pasts,
meditate on our virtues and level of faith.

My young soul is confined between the walls of a house.
A quiet space, a world of my own,
where bravery cannot map an escape,
nor hope can cast its shadow here.

I figured even this seclusion cannot thwart my restlessness.
Stories of a pandemic plague their way into my head.
I feel a fear.
A fear of not knowing the ending.

But when I look on the other side of this heavenly wrath,
I see a silver lining.
The sky above me is healing,
animals have returned to their happy places,
humans are more empathic, more caring,
the value of little moments are now greatly esteemed.
What's the secret beyond this dream-like charm?
Who knows. Who knows.

From the atrophied roots of time-
A prayer rests on my lips.
'Dear Lord,
protect my kindred ones and the world first,
and then protect me.'
That is all I implore.

TRUE COLOURS

Doth thy intent reflect in the mirror?
Doth thy conscience shadow the guilt thou should feel?
Doth thy morals know'st the pain thy deceits inflict?
Or doth thy hide what is real? – Ruth.

By night thou caressed my desires with ardor.
By morrow thou set thy heart on another damsel.
Avaunt thee quoth, we shalt part at thy behest.
My hopes died on fire ever sith, I tholed.

What dost thee take me for? — Fie.
With thy ghost like feelings, fake intent.
Hadst I questioned their candour afore,
Thou would never curdle my blood with fear.

Wonder-Wench! know'st thou not at all?
The forlorn damage thou hath done.
Whenas all thy true colours art bared.
E'en the autumnal tree leaves art dazed.

That lifetime of suppressed emotions,
feel it all-
Let them transcend
beyond space and time-
Into worlds unknown.

PRECIOUS LOVE

Here's to the love you gave me.
Here's to all the times you saved me.
Here's to all the sacrifices you made for my sake.
Here's to all the dangers you harboured in my name.

Frozen in time,
how quiet the loft appears in a moment,
while I clasp a long locked mahogany box, feeling its sturdiness.
Your pictures, your letters, portrait drawings,
withered flowers, heart shaped pendants, the scent of your
perfume-
Keepsakes bestowed by a forbidden love.
There is no need for remorse now, I scarcely think.
Your love was transcendent—
Surreal almost.
I still believe, no one will ever love me the way you did.

You made me your homecoming queen but in vain,
I could never honour you.
I hold scars of my treason to this day,
which I hope I could be forgiven for—
Guilty of dismay against my own heart.
Now paying the price,
for ever having faith that other souls could be like you—
Endearing, with a heart of gold.

How do I ever forget,

when my life seemed to be unravelling like a ball of yarn,
you would pick up the loose ends and gracefully knit them into
hope.
You were fain to accept the hard knocks of my life that repelled
others.

So in all earnest-
Tell the world about precious love, about passion, integrity and
commitment.
Because seemingly they do not know—
A rose has to be loved, with its thorns.
And real beauty is enhanced with its imperfections.

SHARDS OF YOU

When I was a child.
I tripped and fell on broken glass.
My mother hefted me up
and picked the shards from my wounds,
with delicacy and lavender kisses.
She put a dressing on them.
And I felt as good as new.

The love and comfort of her arms relieved the pain immensely.
If only I could tell her how bad I fell for you,
and got hurt along the way-
In very sooth,
she would pick the shards of you,
from my wounded heart,
one at a time.
She would relieve me from the pain
and I would be able to love again.

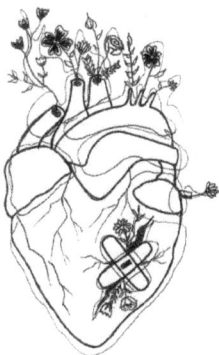

A TRUE TYRANT

The wildfires were put out.
The embers of a dying love flickered,
until the debris was cleared.
Throughout the nightmare of black days and its aftermath,
while I struggled to rebuild and replace what had been
destroyed-
You lived life as a king.
Apologies were burnt out in your kingdom.
My highness-
You could never own up to the wreckage you caused.
All I could hear was your bitter laugh,
hovering darkly over my mourning,
on each smidgen of my sorrow,
you proudly marked your triumph,
with the glory of a true tyrant.

DIACHRONIC YOU

I stitched you together with fragments of my soul.
I collected letters and formed you out of the words I craved.
I connected you with intangible metaphors as a whole.
I weaved a circle of thoughts about you from similes phrased.

Your mind was an elegance of wisdom and creativity.
Your personality glowed with ideas and natural bents.
Your eyes sparkled with mystery and lucidity.
Your tongue was a stardust of jargons and accents.

I poured my entire essence into you, formed you from parts of
myself.
Until I made you sentient, just so you can develop a mind on
your own.
New ideas, new creativity, new beliefs started to emanate from
yourself.
Your assertions and speeches started to change for reasons
unknown.

All I could do was watch my creation shift in your own
wordage.
All I could do was watch you become someone I didn't
recognize anymore.
You changed the locks and added passwords in your own
language.
I do not know you anymore; I do not want to know you
anymore.

- You are no longer a part of me.

APOLOGY

Your flat apology rested on my heart,
like a shipwreck in the depth and gloom of the ocean.
Heavy and worthless-
A second insult, as a coup de grace,
to seal my mouth and submerge your iniquities.
From then on,
my life was nothing,
but a series of apology letters written to myself,
staining the compartments of my heart,
with blues of unspoken words.

I owed myself the biggest apology.
But the word 'sorry' never seemed to overlay the regrets within
me.
Yet I kept on writing those letters.
In the hope of landing on cerulean seabeds,
with no stone of regret
attached to my heart.

The recollection of memories past,
often inspires me to write you in words that,
though icy,
can never match
the glacial coldness in your heart.

GAME OF FLUXX

You played me well like a game of Fluxx.

You set your own rules.

And once I had mastered the characteristics you indicated that

I lacked-

The rules to your game had changed.

There was suddenly something new disappointing you.

DILEMMA

You were both thunderstorm and serenity.
I could not decide whether to run away
or come knocking at your door to find refuge.

DELIRIUM

And the worst part was,
when I was not even worthy of your goodbye.

When you cut me off abruptly.

When you left me in a grotesque delirium,
to wonder if we even parted at all.

HYPOXIA

I did not want to see you in pain.
So I had to let your wish suffocate me every day,
close my airways.
Sweeping over a haze of cerebral hypoxia
and stumble with every smother
into a deeper realm,
until I could easily rip off my lungs-
Just so you could breathe in peace.

HELIOTROPISM

I was inclined to you-
Like the sunflowers move their blooms to face the sun,
instinctively so,
I was bound to find you.
In the same way the sunflowers follow the sun
as it moves across the sky,
every single minute, every waking hour,
I followed your every move.
And much as the sunflowers entrust their evolution to sunlight,
stretching for warmth,
I synchronized my growth with your light.
Without a clue of the noxious shadows you were casting
behind me.

THE SNAKE

You snaked up my body.
Entwined along my spine, wrapped yourself around my tender
marrow.
Slinking so easily as you bestrode me.
Almost like you belonged there.

You slithered over my stomach, devoured butterflies-
So that I would open up to you and clasp you to my bosom.
You did not make me fly but you seeped into my veins.
Infused me with every drop of your poison.
Until all your traits had merged with me.

Devious as you coiled comfortably in my capillaries-
With your forked tongue tied.
You mingled warmly with my blood.
Yet I was the one who carried your venom to my heart.

Your sibilatory stung on my skin-
Like a rattlesnake's kiss before the final bite.
And when you shed your skin, it stuck to me-
Like the poison ivy in my garden.
I kept the remains.
Imprinting the scale traces of your outgrowth.

- I am your new skin.

HOME

The world believes a home is somewhere you could point to on
a map.
A place with a street number.
An address, a postcode.
A house with brick walls & bay windows.
Pouring sunshine like lemon cream-
Through lace heirloom curtains.
Speckling cherry wood floors of a cozy kitchen.
Warm & lavender bubble bath.
Snug beds, soft woolen sheets.
Bedrooms composed of timber photo frames.
Curated collections of memories-
Lining opaline walls.
I believed a home was not a place-
But a feeling of comfort.
And even without a deadbolt to secure,
a latch to pull,
a lock and key,
your arms felt like home.
My safest place-
The closest I could get to heaven.
But the inherent irony of the human condition is this—
We seek people and places to make homes in.
When every day, everywhere, everything changes
and the brick walls close in;
to suffocate all that once made it a home.

WEARY SOUL

Whenever I tried to come close to you with my sweetness,
you gave me only your bitterness.
And this pain that still lingers,
has turned me into a tasteless, weary soul.

CLOSURE

The way we parted feels like burnt open cuts on my skin.
They neither whip into shape.
Nor bury in my flesh.
They remain, they pain, they stain.
Like a time that stands still-
You left with no words of farewell.
Since then, every night,
I send paper planes like wishes soaring into distant skies.
Begging the stars for our peaceful ending.
Just so this abyss of undefined feelings doesn't consume me-
For an eternity.

- I would fight a thousand battles to change the cold-blooded valedictory you chose for us.

PRETENSE

Where do I begin to get rid of everything that you did,
erase the sweet hopes you gave me,
get over the turmoil you left me with?

I unravel the strands of the rope you slashed.
Was it all a pretense?
I don't think I can stand it.

I pull out the strings with my hands-
From a heart that wept for you,
preserving the pain with salt on the wound.

I dream of the plans we used to have.
The dust of something once cherished.
Did it ever matter to you?

And believe me when I tell you,
I meant everything that I said-
From the beginning, till the end.

- I wish I could say the same for you.

THE PIANO

The pull took me inside the mansion.
As I creeped in,
its splendour enveloped even my silhouette.
Mass of maroon antiques,
clasped with costly stones.
Oil painting portraits set in vintage photo frames.
Few grim oak structures.
A colossal French chandelier and relics old-
Bereft since decades.
Dust laid over every surface-
I could sense the memories pulsing
around the peripheral of my mind.
But my eyes were locked on to the grand piano-
served as the centerpiece of one of the rooms.
It had definitely seen better days,
but my urge got the better of me.
Eyes closed, a fervor took over me.
I started playing the pulse;
To the throb of a lost soul-
A lost soul trapped in an unforgiving dry spell
that would never bubble up again.
Or maybe it was just me.
He left, he hasn't come back.
And my fingers felt numb.
He is forever gone, he isn't coming back.
The melody swirled with my heartbeat.

LONELINESS

Loneliness is a place.

And it is not hollow.

It is a cold house devoid of human feelings and warmth,

enclosed by obscured walls,

giving forth echoes of screaming voices.

It has rooms with open windows-

Barred by our own thoughts.

We lean gently out of the sills.

Outside, birches remain aground.

The hills stay rooted.

The sun rises and sets on time.

Days turn into nights and nights turn into days.

We revel in a silent freedom felt only by birds in cages.

Then return to our homely prisons-

To find comfort in the gnawing desolation.

It is all we know.

It is all we feel-

Alone.

If only I could surround him within the chords of my melody.
If only the rhythms could deliver him the message of my restlessness.
If only he could understand the sounds of my heartbeats.
Just once-
Then maybe I would be able to breathe.

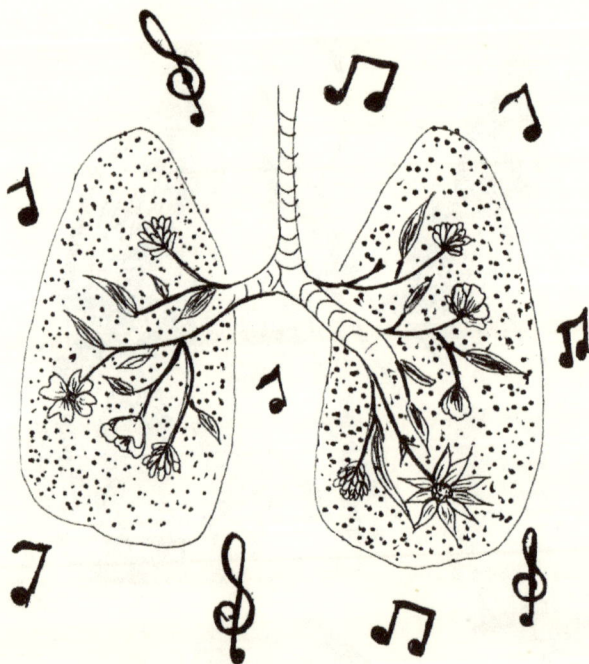

BULLET TRAIN

I catch many trains of thought-
Throughout the day.
Station to station.
Junction to junction.
Taking one track mind,
barreling towards a one-way street,
whooshing past stations of a bygone age.
Backed up memories.
Some come late;
some are dead on arrival.
Most fleeting thoughts never leave.
They never reach a destination.
The end of the line-
Where thoughts remain in quiescent desuetude,
brings a natural closure.
Yet the train never stops-
With its detours and crashes,
gleaming white light at the end,
moving inexorably on at full speed.
But the train is either too early or too late,
lunging between synapses in my brain-
In the fatal crash between the desirable and the unobtainable.

IRISES

When he left,

he not only stepped on the potted irises set on my front porch.

He crushed the tender seedlings.

The little buds we once dreamt of blooming.

He took those dreams with him, together with-

My hopes,

my courage,

my adoration-

Leaving me to hanker after what was never going to be.

SPACETIME

I fall into your spacetime.

Gravity grows stronger.

Black hole, infinite vacuum, pull me closer.

Favonian incalescence-

I cannot escape your deadly comfort.

Tar heart-

I writhe in your dense curvature.

BONFIRE OF THE INNOCENTS

The homes, once the fortresses of love and kinship,
now the woeful hecatombs of living souls,
decimated families-
Leaving children as remnant embers.

I swear they never knew the feeling of homesickness before,
when they wandered aimlessly down a street where they used to
live,
in denial that they would never see their parents again.
Their homes were no longer homes but just rubbles.
Only memories surrounded the places.
They could vividly remember where the tanks stood,
where snippers hid and shot their families dead-
Innocence seeped into the soil below.

Nothing was the same.
Where were their gardens, the olive trees?
Their backyards in which they used to play?
Their rooms, kitchens and porches?
They could not make out the traces.
All were destroyed, burnt to the ground.
And they were just walking over the memories.
Their little hearts were probably sinking.

Who will now comfort them from their nightmares and wipe
their tears?

Who will lovingly prepare their jelly sandwiches for their school meals, place chocolates in their lunch boxes and kiss their little noses before walking them to schools?
Who will touch their foreheads to diagnose fevers;
while melting over the cherubic look in their little eyes staring up?

They have become hapless orphans.
Their parents and siblings are no more.
Their homes cease to exist and there is no way to get them back.
They were just standing there in a suspended moment.
Trying to make sense of their losses.

- Humanity wailed over their innocence.

THE DEVIL'S TRIANGLE

Every dead ship that once sailed within your zone
got hit unexpectedly
by your giant rogue waves.

Your swirling currents
engulfed them
into the darkest profundity.

Just beyond reach.

They suffered your vengeance
for being too naïve,
too vulnerable.

Your dark waters knew no mercy, no boundaries.
They all lost their strengths
and existences.

Just beyond trace.

LIES & EXCUSES

The lies that hung on your tongue,
were they a charade for your truth?

The bogus excuses must have tasted
like acidic seeds in your mouth.

For all the flowers they could not grow,
when you bitterly told me to let go.

BETRAYER

Let's pretend it was not the end of the line.
After crushing my trust, you offered me your friendship.
Should I give away a fortune to a greedy chasm?
Or dance around your room like an orbiting planet?
You should have known better.
A boon does not come from generous fountains and sweet milk.
Love and faith have borne the cost.
We are not a taste you can sweeten anymore.
Milk turns sour when left out for hours.
Spoiled.

- How do I befriend my betrayer?

CONSTELLATIONS

He was made with a space void inside him.
The kind of vacuity which can never be filled.
His heart was an empty place aged by light-years.
And I was foolishly tracing constellations
over fractals
of him and I.

CELESTIAL BODIES

By the time I kept afloat the vacuum around the space,
nauseated over all cosmic mirages,
He was the earth-
Weighing towards my orbit.
Grabbing my waist,
pulling me into his comforting gravity
with no astronomical extravagance, no chaotic motion.
Together, we were in orbit.
And I was convinced,
somewhere, someone was charting the movement of our
celestial bodies.

SHOW AND TELL

After making me fall for you,
you decided you were better off alone.
Your show and tell,
the ace that fell out your sleeve,
place a faulty mirror on my eyes
of what you made me believe you were.
Bloody ocean wish me well,
as I drown your memory down under.

PURPLE MOODS

Purple moods make you swoon.

Take my crimson red love and leave me blue.

My skin will turn cold in your embrace.

I was willing to forget every bad deed tied to your name.

I've let you hide my feelings under the ground.

I'm digging up their roots and planting more.

THE DEMON

You could rise to the threshold of the heavens-
Claim innocence to every sin you made.
And every trick you played.
But what good would it do?
You can't hide your bloody skin.
Your demonic horn.
Your crooked feet.

- Demons cannot be backtracked.
And misdeeds cannot be camouflaged.

The gravity that pulls my soul to you-
Dilates.
Your beauty slows time.
Even if the world turned grey,
your beauty would fill my eyes,
like dazzling arrays of colours-
In a kaleidoscope.

YOUR PRISM

Every time the season changes,
you consider another change of heart.
And the pain you leave me in,
always gets refracted into your prism,
scattering my identity to places-
In rays of insipidness, unworthiness and ugliness.

- I can't figure out which one of the rays hurts the most.

COSMIC YOU

You are a home of spiral galaxies,
held by a gravity,
firm enough to equilibrate your permanence.
You contain a myriad of shining stars
and a moon as a chandelier.

I know how difficult it is for you to see your wonder from afar.
But all the burning asteroids that hit you
and the nebulae that clouded up your senses,
they all brought you a stellar grace to conquer your space.

So whenever you feel like your stars are collapsing,
know that you have a slew of supernovae up your sleeves.
They will disperse light and energy
to form bones of stardust,
giving birth to a new you.

This is change, breaking until the pieces form something new.
At this stage, no more black holes should lay claim to you.
For you already carry everything within yourself.
You need no one to call you strong or powerful,
because you behold this in you,
an entire universe.

QUANTUM CHROMODYNAMICS

The universe is full of quarks and gluons.
But darling, I never bow down to them.
You must know,
I let no one exploit my asymptotic freedom.
Not even you.

LIMINAL SPACE

You remained for a while on the horizon.
Then you vanished without saying a word.
Your light was gone.
I was left stranded in bleak oblivion.
Somewhere between daylight and darkness.
I try to unleash myself out of these shadows.
But time dissolves differently for me.
More slowly, more painfully.
And the future asserts uncertainty-
Hovering above me like a dark cloud.
An eerie reminder of an unrevealed spectre.

The solemn room was filled with an endless pit of darkness.
As I snuck in,
struggling to breathe.
A labour of love and intense pain
took me to bath you
and bundle you in a shroud,
perfumed with incense.
When it came to surrendering your body to the Almighty,
I was left to place my heart in your shroud.
Because your bones and flesh
were not enough
to make a child's shroud
as fit as it should be.

Of all the lives and universe.
Of all the true relations of the heart.
Of all the stories and fables.

You left me in the one-
I have to survive without you.

THE BUTTERFLY

Your smile fitted onto
your cheek line.
Like a butterfly,
spread out its wings
in all its glory.

You stared at me.
The butterfly waited,
wings outspread.
I could only hope
I smiled back tentatively.

"Look here" (in your eyes)
You asked me.
Your eyes warmed as they met mine.
The butterfly was in my bosom.
I wish I could seize
that one moment
in my clasp.

You,
You only smiled.
The butterfly took flight.

HIDDEN GLORY

A silhouette from the past
stealing rain from the icy grey sky.
Pitter patter on the woodland-
Flashes before my eyes.
Here I stand again in front of a waterfall.
As I look through the blue sapphire waters of the lake.
Crystallized of a frosted memory-
I see you.
Sitting on a rock.
You always revel in nature.
But you were gazing at me instead.
A hidden glory thereof springs forth-
The kind I've longed to see return.

Nowhere in this world,
have I seen anyone
looking at someone-
The way you look at me.

If I knew I could bleed so much
from trying to smooth a stone,
I would have left it as I first found it-
Hard and dry.

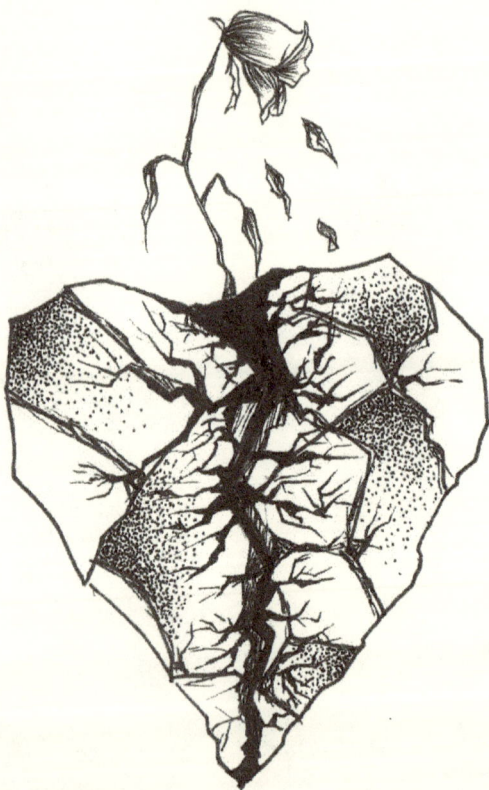

SUFFERING

When I became transfixed by your sweet nothings
and feathery promises-
Reality felt like a strained grip.
You tried to confine me to suffering.
But I just had no connection to sufferings.
Suffering has its roots in existence-
I had no existence.

PATH

My path was that which was yours.
Then you decided to leave.
Once more we went on separate paths.
I found a beautiful path, effortless.
But I only wandered into it for a time-
Since your memories kept coming along like a mirage.
And the destination seemed tainted.

HEAVEN ON EARTH

The passing of time keeps growing ever longer.

Older joys fade and wit her to weeds.

The trails of departed footsteps are untraceable.

Echoes of forgotten talks are too faint to be recalled anymore.

Some memories used to be 'heaven on earth' -

Now they are just beneath it.

RAINBOW

As I entered glistening portals into lands unknown,
those ghostly routes entangled me.
I was only ever offered the shadows.
Never the hidden raw truths-
Till I saw a rainbow of distant hues,
revealing a completely different view.

*- From those eerie shadows to those true colours, nature brings
everything to light.*

AT PEACE

An invisible thread connected me to you,
indifferent to where it actually led.
Even when I was sitting alone-
I was still at peace.

- *Your absence distorts reality.*

A LOFTY PRINCESS

There was once a lofty princess.
Spellbound by her charms and soaring heights,
a score of knights used to come to her castle.
They all sung praises to her,
danced with her gracefully.
Her innocent face could smite the lousiest of devils they said.
But she knew nothing at all-
They were actually devils who came as knights
and left as devils.

NEVER QUITE FADING

She had walked back to the place she once thought was her
home,
ever since her love was forever gone.
She retraced those steps she once took with him.
Into a grove where lemon trees used to grow-
Only to find burnt cinder ashes and memories drifting through
air.
Never quite fading-
Yet never remaining.
And then she started to wonder if that place she thought was
home
was even home at all.

BURNED HOME

This home has burned down.
The crackling of wasted arguments and accusatory tones roars
in my ears.
The smell of charcoaled love and care burns my sinuses.
The taste of smoky curse words makes me cough.
The sight of heavy fights scorches my eyes.
And the worst part is no one understands any of this,
but me.

HEARTSICK

I'm heartsick of wishes left unspoken.

Remorseful of unlived moments.

I wait enduringly for faith to translate to truth.

For my heart to know what it has never truly known.

But none of it has been felt yet.

And what is not felt is everlasting-

So how will I ever finish grieving?

LIVING GHOST

A moment evolved into a memory.
Only then I realized that I could have rejoiced in it a little more.
For once I felt at peace when you held me in your arms.
Now you are just a living ghost,
holding some other woman in your arms.
Intangible as a nightmare.

LACHRYMOSE EYES

'Look at my lachrymose eyes.'
I said to him-
'They have known only pain.'

'Your eyes are incredible.'
He replied-
'Even in their pain, they look like florals and kindness.'

YOUR VIOLENCE

I bear my skin for you
and blood oozes from it.
If I could connect all the blood drops,
they would make up a constellation of untold stories
and your violence would narrate themselves.

ONE SPLIT SECOND

Can the clock slow down time?
Like a traveler who takes rests during his journey-
To make something last longer.
Unwanted moments linger.
Desirable moments speed up and slip beyond one's grasp.
Is this the paradoxical beauty of a blessing or a curse?
Either or both-
We never know.
All it takes is one split second for everything to fall into place.
And all it takes is one split second for everything to fall
a p a r t.

Home is deemed to be a place that makes you forget the worldly chaos.
My home turned out to be the worldly chaos.

SOUL-MATES

Do not lament on your relationships that have failed.
Your love schemes that have proved to be illusions.
But like a brave warrior, bid farewell to them.
And have faith-
For once, true love will seem possible.
And it won't be related to life and death.
It won't be bound to the body nor a lifetime-
But to the soul.
Soulmates do not magically meet somewhere.
They were made and linked to each other in the realm of souls-
Since the beginning of time.
And for decades to come, they would find each other here too.

You are a mountain river.
Let no one build a dam across you.
You were created to gush without impulse-
Not to stay enclosed.

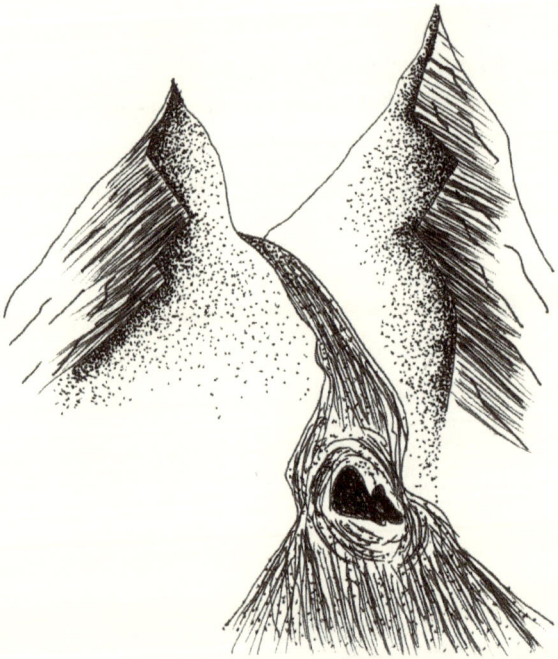

YOUR BLOWS

There's a song by Halsey on repeat in my mind.
A memory from ice cold days-
When I was immured in your car.
And your blows set their roots in narratives under my skin-
Into blue pieces.
Until that stops too,
goosebumps will prickle on my skin.

LEARNED HELPLESSNESS

They say you'll never be happy
if you don't let go of the things that make you sad.
But what if the things that make you sad
are holding onto you?

Victimhood tells a story that has a flipside.
You feel enslaved by your trauma.
You can't see any exit even when
you are suffocating in a dark place
and the door is wide open,
you don't even try to leave
because you've come to believe that you can't.

Your state of mind is spawned from trauma.
You endure an aversive stimulus and you feel unable to evade.
So like a big elephant held back by a puny rope.
When in reality it is held by its belief.
It has the force to break away from the rope but for some
reason it doesn't. Because it was tied to the same rope when
it was young and it couldn't break free. So the elephant grew
up with the belief that the rope is still strong to restrain it.
Likewise you are held back by your own beliefs that make you
incapable to escape from your pasts and traumas.

But here's a kernel of truth-
You have the power in you to break away from everything that

is seeking to hold you hostage.
You just need a little pull.
Take a step and start making choices to unlearn this survival response
and the false boundaries created by the past.
This will only happen when you learn self-responsibility.
You learn that you are more worthy than what has happened to you.
You may have more to the story of your trauma.
But embrace healing-
It gives another story,
with a better ending.

REALITY

I thought I could live the way I dream.

When crimson skies unfold a whimsical day.

Dancing wild flowers in harmony of the breeze.

You and I running errands in the lush wheat fields.

Basking in cherry sunsets, laughter and bird songs.

We sit by a mill pond.

You whisper to me-

'The way our hearts are beating right now, this is immortality.'

For one moment, there seemed not to be any sorrow in the world.

Until reality came knocking at my door.

- When reality strikes, dreams become long-dashed.

If there was ever a miracle that walked this earth,
then
it's you.

He is the first light of the universe.
His glory and grace are anchored in eternity.
He is the one whose kindness opens doors in the sky
and makes God's qualities visible.
Not a single soul could rival him in humility.

Nothing truly beautiful can ever take form on earth after him.
Bestowed upon him,
are miracles that transcend the span of human imagination-
To cure every affliction.
Nature was rapt in wonder by his goodwill.
The palm trees yearned for him,
stones greeted him and
the moon was cleft asunder for him.

He is from God and we, from him.
He showed us the path of life.
Know that if you are willing to find the realm of eternal truth,
and divine love,
it is his light you must seek.
And if you are willing to find him,
follow the path that leads to the immortal land,

where lofty palaces are made in gardens of everlasting bliss,
gardens greater than the expanse of this earth,
underneath which rivers of milk and honey flow.
Wait for him there.

The perpetuity of your being
has been preserved in the
marrow of my soul.

- You will live in me until the day I die.

A PEARL

She was a pearl
hidden inside a shell
in the deep bottom,
wondering where the ocean is.
When all along-
The ocean was her home.

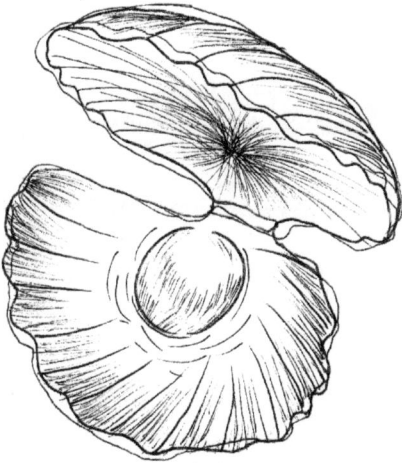

I tried to break free from his despicable clutch.

I was left stranded in my own consciousness.

His demons won't let me get close to the truth I needed the most.

I tried to speak but it was not within my reach.

Have you seen a fish gasping on land, near the water?

Yet it can't move back to the water.

Helplessness has it at chokehold.

The fish suffocates out of the water.

I suffocated in it.

It lasted for a while.

Until the sun was here.

The shore came to me.

And I finally got my head above water.

OCEAN CHILD

Take her to the ocean,
where the vastness of the midnight blue water
stretches in every direction to the horizon,
sun rays are broken into mosaic of reflected iridescence over the
surface,
corals and reefs are pastel coloured palaces of sea creatures
and dolphins do graceful aquatic dance.

Take her to the ocean,
Where her pulse is in synchrony with the pulse of the waves,
the rhythm of the water salves her caged heart
and her soul intermingles with a second universe of life.
There only will she find her haven.
There only will she find freedom.

BARRIERS

The barrier where the lagoon and the open sea meet,
is the exact barrier which separates them.
The area between them is filled with beauty.
And the lagoon can be adjacent to the open sea but they will
never mix.
If they do, sea creatures will suffer.
So the barrier ensures that neither tries to take over the other.
And the beauty exists for they don't become one.

- Some barriers are best if never dissolved.

YOUR LEGACY

Your heart flutters.
Your strength falters.
The cruel world has viciously reduced you to a quivering wreck.
Yet kindness majestically dangles a golden chain around your neck.
You warrior queen-
Wear it proudly as a medallion for your sufferings.
The universe won't ever know you until your wounds and scars are seen.
This is your legacy.
It is easy to possess the milk of kindness when life treats you kind.
It is integrity to stay kind when it treats you rough.
Recall your imperial armours in honour of the gift of life-
To outlive an anguish that might never cease.
To proceed with patience and fortitude under sufferings.
To stay gentle in the face of tribulation.
For true virtue is your crown forged from moral strength,
honesty,
and good faith.

IRIDESCENCE

Deep and refined feelings echoed from silent voices.
To express them would somehow taint their sincerity.
Love was devotion for iridescence and secret glances.
She expressed it, messy and lovely-
In a color trail of pastel shades.
Anticipating them to disperse into enchanting rainbows.
Like the gentle hush of colours allaying her cold dying soul.
Twisted in sparkling beauty through dripping walls.
Nothing spelled of remorse-
Because nothing was left to rue for.
Everything whispered of grace among the hues.
All were clarity and natural daydreams.

DECEPTIVE PARADOX

The earth is round,
doesn't mean it's having
a ball.

Waves crash,
doesn't mean they aren't
in control.

The sea is deep,
doesn't mean
it is thoughtful.

Two lands meet,
doesn't mean
they aren't in war.

And you wonder how people can be deceptive?

GRAVITATIONAL PULL

I never thought I could need anyone to function.
Like the sun, I let planets orbit around me-
Fearless,
maverick,
autarchic.
A tempestuous ball of fire.
Then you came into my life
and forthwith, I became the spring tides.
And you, my moon-
My existence,
my strength,
the rise and fall of my soul
depended solely on you.

INTEGRITY

What is integrity but grace in the face of adversity?

The roots that never had to fight for the sun and the sky in rainforests
will always grow into beautiful trees.

The roots that encroach through concrete and strong wind
are the ones that can outgrow and withstand dangers untold.

TRUST YOUR VIBES

The path you're walking on may not seem aligned with where you want to reach.
You may have a heavy cross to bear.
And your plans may not be set in stone yet.
But in all circumstances, trust your vibes.
They draw your soul to everything which contributes to unfold your most glorious traits.
All you need is to give in.

TRANSFORMATION

Beauty is the way a butterfly
flaps its crystalline wings
and reveals the colours of spring.

But it too had to escape
from its cocoon and transform
its world.
So will you.

- Trust the process.

YIN AND YANG

There may be two people who experience the same trauma
but one will be haunted by it
and the other one will be free from any scars.

It is not the events in your life that mold you,
but your interpretations to those events.
Our lives alternate between happiness and pain.

If you find meaning in the pain and
see it as an opportunity to grow and learn,
you will overcome the obstacles and embrace the challenges in
life.

You could go through many tests and trials,
but if you understand the wisdom of those trials,
then you'll master your emotions.

Remember everything in nature is created with a harmonious
balance.
The give-and-take of energy, the ebb and flow
of all existences exist in the most stable equilibrium.

Just like the darkness and light.
The chaos and calm.
The yin and yang.

IMMORALITY

So engrossed are they in an immorality-
the negative of righteousness and grace,
that committing it appears remarkably normal to them,
as long as it matches their own moral interest.
albeit unethical.

TRUST NOTHING

If you should ask me what to trust,

My answer is-

nothing.

The love that you protect, also has the power to destroy you

Just like,

The land that holds the skyscrapers, also has the power to make

them

c

r

u

m

b

l

e

IN MOTION

She never embraced the conventional way of living.
Never surrendered to the weight of disappointments
and fortuitous losses.
She was born to be in motion.
She always yearned for new discoveries.
Even after every hopeless misadventure,
she would look for new horizons to find her way-
Because she never believed in dead ends,
but in only new ways to start a life.

EMPATHY

Feel the one you can understand.

Make the one you can feel a part of you.

Bond with their pain.

Live their pain.

When both pains will coalesce, both worlds will coalesce.

Time will change.

Circumstances will change.

And the balance of nature will be restored.

RESILIENCY

The pillars of strength and patience
do not consist in formalities,
rather in the moral discipline and belief
that we are made of such undeniable resiliency
to not only endure trials
and challenges,
but also to proceed with courage
in the face of afflictions
on the way we choose,
in accordance with the dictates of our own conscience.

Every step I take makes the floorboard creek.
Tiptoe towards the unknown.
Illume my bounds.
Distances between hearts are lessened with love.

WATER UNDER THE BRIDGE

Say goodbye to the days behind with no remorse, no guilt.
Wade into the flowing river.
Journey towards the meadow that holds your euphoria.
Live for the moment, seize it and make it count.
The rest is just water under the bridge.

MILESTONES

I used to tell my mother-
'Your daughter,
physically impaired,
would never reach those milestones.'

Today my mother looked at me and said,
'My darling,
you've defied those milestones.'

THE LIGHT UPON LIGHT

Death is nothing but a bridge that joins you to your true
Beloved,
from the realm of material to the realm of attainment.
Work on building a state of unity with Him
and you'll fly with spiritual wings to that place.
That place which has no beginning and no end.
That place where there is none other than the effulgence of His
essence.
The light upon light.

LIVING IN PIECES

When you learn the ways of the wild,
you learn what it means to be flawed,
don't you see?
We always wilt before we grow.
And as I lie here,
while the falling leaves are gracing me,
wilting wildflowers.
I realize for the first time that;
living in pieces,
is still living.

GRIEF

Grief is all the unrealized love
we hold for someone,
escaping our soul in tears and heartache.

The dilemma is the infinite love we carry,
which spurs the grief.

TRUE LOVE

It's not always
going to be
effervescent, sparkling or
bungee jumping
love.

Sometimes it's
about being dull
and lifeless
together.

But
come hell or
high water,
true love
doesn't have
a death.
It outlasts
Anything.
Everything.

THE SOURCE

It is not the nature of things or
the pleasure of this world to satisfy us,
but the awakening of the heart
that needs to find its way to the divine truth,
the Oneness,
the goal of the quest.
Every circumstance and
detail of your life which draw you to the
origin of faith are the true pleasures.
Your heart is enlivened
when it knows wisdom and faith-
the magnets that pull you to the source.
Only then will you attain inner purity.
Only then will you reach the level of truth-
your purpose.

- He created the creation so He would be known.

EARTHLY TIES

All the earthly ties and vanity
that you so adore,
all the things that bring you
insignificant pleasures,
those in which you search for
your identity and worth,
all of them will shackle you.
You'll find out they come with a price.

- « So let not the worldly life deceive you. » 35:5

HIS LIGHT

It is not the stars
that guide me,
but His light.

His light permeates
my broken soul,
filling every crack.

In the creeks between
tribulation and rapture,
strength

c
a
s
c
a
d
e
s

LEAVE

If he ever has to measure
the love he has for you
based on who you are,
what you can offer him,
and how you can enhance his image,
l e a v e.
Love can be many things,
but it is never on trial.

DARLING

Darling, can't you see?
We were made of the same stardust,
melded so intimately together
that we spark the souls of each other.

Darling, behold.
The lines on your palms meet with mine.
We would exist so wholly together.
How could we not cross paths?

Darling, tell me?
Do you see yourself in the same light that I do?
Because I can't even compare you to anyone.
You are a transcendental entity.

BLOOD MOON

The blood moon ascends
from behind the mountains,
emulous over us,
we bathe in its
celestial musk.
And I wonder,
You look like royalty
in this scarlet red hour.

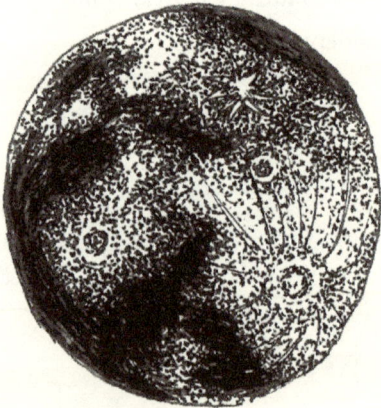

THE GUARDIAN; THE WITNESS; THE OVERSEER

I would never know that people could be monsters,
had You not stripped off their layers,
one by one until I felt the pain.

I would never know poisonous arrows sprung from bows
could be detached from human hearts,
until You mended my heart.

I would never be aware of the strength I possess,
unless my life had not become a testament to Your promise-
'You do not burden a soul beyond that it can bear'.

And I would definitely not know that
You could save me from greater tragedies and bring me relief
when I tied knots of Your oaths to my heart.

But now I know that Your Love and care
hold our lives and everything in the universe,
with the most impeccable balance at all times.

You are God's finest creation.
An archetype of beauty.
Not any mediocre construct.
You were crafted in the best of moulds.
Not in haste, not in error.
Your beauty was known to God before you even existed-
This is your liberty to be yourself.
Monopolize your self-worth.
Let not society's idea of
physical attractiveness
inhibits you from loving
the flesh covering your bones.

You can't possibly untangle
the life of another person
when yours is despairingly knotted.

- Start with yourself first.

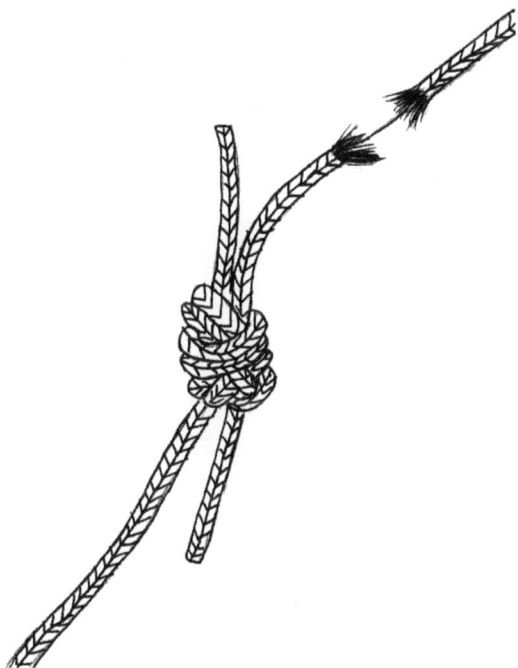

EXALTED ARE YOU

You love me as You find me.
And I owe it to You-
To honour the love and mercy
You have showered upon me.
Exalted are You-
In the face of my heart's worst fears,
in every pang of sorrow,
and unfair cruelty,
You taught me how to thrive.
So now I keep breathing in gratitude
into my lungs,
by whispering your names-
the 99 praises.

FORCE OF NATURE

Her devotion faced a blazing farewell,
still smoldering, regardless
of the concomitant ashes.
But she always learned to take fire as it is,
and wouldn't even protect herself.
Even still what was left, seemed more brutally
and beautifully honest,
she was a flamboyant force of nature.

An hourglass is sometimes
just a transparent arbitrary
held in a fair conjunction,
and I can still taste the gunpowder I swallowed
when you timed our last conversation
that was going to be wound up
centuries deep anyway.

- *His claws of terror.*

LIFE

Grief makes riddles out of us.

It makes us feel weak trying to hold heavy days together.

But you beautiful soul-

If you feel like you need to fall,

let yourself fall.

It is a good time to contemplate your existence

and strengthen your core.

After that, take heart.

Pick yourself again.

Reconnect with yourself.

Reclaim your power that you have doled out to people who

didn't deserve it.

And embrace growth, like a flower.

A flower grows from nothing, with wavering hopes.

Yet they still do.

You may be plucked, stamped on, strewn aside by reckless

hands,

but your roots are still strong and retained by the earth to be

resurrected.

Look into the burning sun that sets the sky ablaze with fiery

reds

and sparks of life,

you will see-

There is always a new beginning,

a new chapter,

a new story waiting to be discovered.

It's a whole new world every single day.
Take each new day at a time,
and delve into it through different possibilities.
Life is as fleeting as a soap bubble.
You never know when it can burst into nothingness.
So bathe your heart and soul in your ambitions
and pave your own path with the dreams you sow.
I assure you-
It will be fruitful.

SHAKA

Is it your ardent gaze emanating galaxies?
Is it the tint and hues in those hazel and ocean eyes radiating
endless love?
Is it your selflessness, your sweet honeycomb heart;
for accepting to share what was once only yours, your whole
world.
Is it the way you talk;
with your wholesome woofs?
Is it the affectionate cuddles or your constant need of attention?
Could it be your playful ways?
Perhaps the innocence in your mischiefs?
Or maybe because you bring everyday sunshine?
I wouldn't know.
But I do know that I love you.
I love you in my own endless way,
a certain breathless way,
a *husky* way.

HONESTY

Sweet girl,
be with the man who wears honesty like a crown,
who carries the fear of God in his heart,
so you won't have to worry
about having the earth to quake beneath your feet,
nor about being caught in quicksand,
slowly and painfully sinking
d

     o

         w

            n

SUNFLOWER

You have the soul of the sunflower.
Buzzing sunshine aureate.
Even with your faulty growth and wilted heart,
know that you are a reminder of the uplifting sun,
and as long as there is light in this world,
there will still be light within you.

As this new season comes forth,
may you find an elysian sky full of sunshine and rainbows.
The hurricanes you have tamed were not overcame in vain,
and I hope it makes sense now.

May you embrace all the blessings that have bloomed for you.
I hope you finally understood why it rained ceaselessly.
This is your new season to bloom.
Steal the happiness from every moment and bloom with
elegance.

May you find the strength to forgive your past and all the
people in it.
I hope your forgiveness frees the chains attached to your heart
and quells the thirst of your wounds.
I wish you faith to believe that there is still more joy to be had.

And at last, may you find an eternity of the truest love.
The tears you have cried have washed away your hurt.
I admire you for what you have patiently endured.
Your weary heart is now healed and freed.

LESSONS LEARNED

1- People will turn out to be monsters, no matter how well you may think you know them but you can't really blame the monsters for being what they have always been, nor are we entitled to be treated gracefully. People are free to be what they want, good or evil. It's up to you to choose what to allow in your life, it's up to you to guard your happiness. Only you have the steering wheel of your life, it's up to you to adjust your sail.

2- Nobody owes you anything. Nobody owes you any happiness, everyone creates his own happiness, and everyone feels his own happiness. Nobody owes you good moral conduct. It's nobody's duty to tend to your life concerns. Surely they can if they want to, but that doesn't mean they are bound to. However bitter this may sound, this is how the world works. You are your own person. You are independent. Drop down your silent expectations on people.

3- You can place the world at the feet of some people, they will still be ungrateful. But hold no grudges. It's such a fulfilling thing to give without any expectation of receiving back.

4- Be kind but remember kindness does not mean to allow yourself to be covered in dirt, be bullied and used.

5- Some days you will have everything and some days you will remember what it feels to have everything but in both circumstances, stay grateful.

6- Often you'll find yourself in a place where all the roads will lead you towards your death, you just have to find that fire inside you which makes you want to live and build it up into strength and get over what was becoming the end of you. It's in there.

7- The universe has been molded on chaos and chaos is part of life but if you lose yourself at the sight of it, you lose your ability to subdue it. Work on building a safe haven inside yourself and the chaos in the external world won't be able to reach it.

8- People will always try to destroy your peace. But know that these people are not worth your time. Don't linger in their games and fakeness. Detach yourself from what's not worthy of you. Stand fearless. Condition your mind in such a way that you are no longer afraid of losing people.

9- Connect with yourself, accept that there are things beyond your control. Just trust the process and surrender yourself to the fact that the outcome will be how it is meant to be.

10- No one is going to save you, no one is supposed to. The only person who will save you already exists within you.

11- All you have is your present, breathe life into it. Nothing is certain. Don't try to revive the past, it is already dead. Don't drool for the future, it is nothing but a pipe dream. The future is real, yes. You might witness it, you might not as well.

12- This world is a masquerade. People do their best to come across as perfect. They forget who they even really are beneath the noise and clutter. They try to sugarcoat their pain especially when they are worried to be left out. But being vulnerable has never equaled being weak. Being raw, honest and vulnerable is the only way you can allow the universe to heal through you.

13- If you need to let anything guide you in this life, let it be your faith and your truth.

REDEMPTION

The sun is up.
The crystal water laps at my feet.
The trees chuckle and whisper my name.
The flowers are velvet and blooming.
Time is now awakened and ticking.
My heart is thawed.
My fading scars gleam a satisfying kind of red.
And my days are bearers of spring and love.
I am happy, like the sun rises in a summer sky.
Hope fills my chest as I breathe in a rainbow of emotions.
I finally found a safe place to call home.
I am living the best days of my life.

It is the day when the world does not have to feign beauty.
White-feathered doves lay upon pillows of silk,
pansies pirouette scatter their blooms all around.
The trees effortlessly blend through birdsongs-
To the glorious riches that come from heaven,
distilling out empyrean irradiance-
You are the sky above where my soul lives.
I stare into your spectral blush pink and lavender hues,
whilst the wind delivers me your message-
'You are mine,
forever.'

ACKNOWLEDGEMENTS

My deepest gratitude goes to everyone at Leaf Publishing House who worked on Hiraeth. I'm highly indebted to Adil. His interest and enthusiasm to make this book possible never lagged and is appreciated.

Last but not least, thank you dear reader for being part of this journey. I pray that it helps and inspires you in some way or another. I wish you, all the love and strength you need to move through the circle of life. Stay full of hope. Stay full of faith. Stay full of love.

www.ingramcontent.com/pod-product-compliance
Lightning Source LLC
Chambersburg PA
CBHW030457100426
42813CB00002B/252